Jaso

MAD®
CLOBBERS The CLASSICS

Written by
LARRY SIEGEL
Illustrated by
ANGELO TORRES
Edited by
Nick Meglin

WARNER BOOKS

A Warner Communications Company

WARNER BOOKS EDITION

Copyright © 1981 by Larry Siegel, Angelo Torres
and E.C. Publications, Inc.

All rights reserved.
No part of this book may be reproduced without permission.
For information address E.C. Publications, Inc.,
485 Madison Avenue, New York, N.Y. 10022

Title "MAD" used with permission of its owner.
E.C. Publications, Inc.

This Warner Books Edition is published by
arrangement with E.C. Publications, Inc.

Warner Books, Inc.,
75 Rockefeller Plaza,
New York, N.Y. 10019

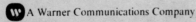 A Warner Communications Company

Printed in the United States of America

First Printing: September, 1981

10 9 8 7 6 5 4 3 2 1

TABLE OF CLASSICS

A stirring sea saga of one man's compulsion to find and destroy the great brooding aristocrat of all white whales...

MOPEY DUKE

by Helmsman Marvel

My name is Fishmael. Like many American boys growing up in the early 19th century, I had always had a restless desire for adventure. But in my case it was a bit stronger than most. The sea was in my blood.

Often-times at night I would lie awake listening to the haunting sound of the waves beating down on my pulmonary vein while a lonely gull would flap its wings against my aorta, and my brother, Phineas, who shared my bed, reeled in sardines with a bent safety pin through my esophagus.

I could hold back the urge no longer, and so one day I decided to leave home and go out to sea. My parents were greatly distraught by my decision.

"*You* become a sailor?" my father scoffed. "Hah! Look at you, you don't even have a wooden leg. You *know* all 19th century sailors have wooden legs. What would the Petersons next door say?"

"That's true," said my mother. "Them with their boy, Pegleg, out in the Pacific, and their other son, Gimpy, at Annapolis."

"We'd be the laughing stock of the neighborhood," said my father. "And not only don't you have a wooden leg..."

"I know, I know," I said. "I don't own a parrot."

"Son," said my mother, "*all* sailors have parrots."

"I'll get a job," I promised. "I'll make money and buy a parrot. Then I'll become a sailor."

"Not without a wooden leg," my father reminded me.

"You can't break up a set," my mother warned.

I pleaded with them. I said someone has to begin *somewhere*. I offered to start small. I'd sprain my foot, find a sparrow, and join the Coast Guard. But they wouldn't hear of it.

However I was not to be denied. I ran away from home, went to New Bedford, and signed on as an apprentice seaman on the whaling ship *Kumquat*.

I turned out to be a great sailor, and life at sea was everything I had dreamed it would be. I worked 22 hours a day, threw up every 45 minutes, and my back was flogged regularly by the first mate's bullwhip. I was a great sailor, but a terrible dreamer.

Yes, life was grueling aboard the *Kumquat,* and tempers were short. As my 50 fellow seamen clumped alongside me on their wooden legs, they were constantly griping about the inhumane work schedule and the cruelty of the first mate. "What does he want from us?" one cried. "How much more can a body take?"

"That's right," said another. "After all, we're only flesh and wood."

But the back-breaking work went on and so did the griping. "Do you realize we have to swab this deck 24 hours a day?" one of the sailors said. "How can you *possibly* keep a deck clean?"

"For one thing," I said, finally losing my temper, "you can get rid of those 50 God-damned parrots!"

I immediately regretted my outburst, when I was almost torn limb from limb by 12 enraged sailors and four hot-headed birds.

And so life went on. Then during our fifth day at sea, we finally met the skipper, Captain Aycrab, for the first time. He was a short, wizened man with scraggly hair, and we could see at once what a fearful toll his long years of battling whales had taken. Not only did he have a wooden leg, but also a wooden arm, a wooden neck, and a wooden ear. There was something else unusual about him. When I took a closer look, I could see what it was. Perched on his shoulder was a wooden parrot.

He fed the bird a wooden cracker and then he spoke to us.

"Mates," he said, "there are many whales out there on the deep, but our concern is with just one. Mopey Duke, the legendary white whale. I have been tracking him down now, man and boy, for nigh unto 50 years. Finding him is my one overwhelming passion in life. I must get him! I must!"

"What will you do when you find him, Captain?" asked a sailor.

Suddenly Captain Aycrab's eyes flashed like twin stabs of lightning. "There has been a prophesy," he said.

A wave of medieval fear and superstition engulfed the vessel.

"A prophesy," echoed a sailor.

"A prophesy," parroted a bosn's mate.

"A prophesy, whistle, whistle, squawk, squawk," parroted a parrot.

"It was a prophesy," the captain went on, "handed down to me many, many years ago by a venerable sage in Tibet. And now I shall repeat that prophesy. Here is the prophesy."

As we stood there in awed silence he reached into his pocket, took out a small shell-like pastry, cracked it open, removed a piece of paper, and read, "You will make many friends because you are trustworthy, loyal, helpful, friendly, courteous, kind, obedient, cheerful, thrifty, brave, clean, and reverent."

"Wrong prophesy," he said, throwing it away, and reaching into his pocket again. He took out another slip of paper, and once more he spoke, "Here is the prophesy: You will spend the rest of your life in a determined quest for a great white whale. And when you find him…"

He paused dramatically as we awaited his next words breathlessly. Then he continued, "…you will kill him single-headedly."

He stared at us long and hard, and then saying, "All right, mates, dismissed," he started to hobble away.

I thought for a moment, then I rushed up to him. "Excuse me, Captain," I said. "You said, 'kill him single-headedly.' Isn't the expression supposed to be, 'single-*handedly*?'"

His fiery eyes pierced mine, and he reached into his pocket and took out another slip of paper. Then he read me another prophesy from the same venerable sage: "You will tell all smart-ass sailors not to screw around with prophesies."

He told me and limped away.

The days passed and the *Kumquat* proceeded on its dedicated mission to find Mopey Duke, the great white whale. We sailed the seven seas, made the strenuous voyage around the Cape of Good Hope, risked the treacherous waters around Cape Horn, and of course, most difficult of all, took the torturous trip through Panama. "Some day," the captain vowed, "they will build a canal through this jungle, and it will be a lot easier on our ship."

We encountered nothing but frustration on our endless voyage. We came across black whales, grey whales, green whales, yellow whales, and orange whales. We even got a fleeting glimpse of Dougie, a mincing fuchsia whale, who had only recently come out of the water closet. But no white whale!

We were forced to do battle with some of these specimens, and Captain Aycrab paid the price. Soon he not only had a wooden neck and ear, but two wooden legs, two wooden arms, a wooden hip, and a wooden duodenum.

During my long years as a sailor I have experienced many agonizing moments, but I can say in all truth that the most dreadful, the most poignant of all is when a badly wounded seaman lies on deck and emits the heart-chilling scream: "Carpenter! Carpenter!"

Half-way through our fifth year at sea, morale on board the ship was at its lowest point. Rations were almost non-existent, the crew was exhausted, and most horrifying of all, except for his nose, Captain Aycrab was now reduced to a solid block of wood.

"How is he?" I asked the carpenter one day, dropping in at the infirmary.

The carpenter sighed. "As well as can be expected," he said. "He's responding to treatment. But..."

"But?" I said.

The carpenter shook his head sadly. "I don't like the looks of that nose."

Deciding to get a second opinion, he called in another carpenter, and a decision was reached. The nose would have to go.

Since there was very little available wood to spare, the carpenters did the next best thing. They grafted a long, sharp, beak-shaped chunk of iron to the middle of the captain's face. "Now see that he gets plenty of rest," said the head carpenter. "Polish him every four hours, and if there are any problems, call me in the morning."

The voyage continued, and then it happened. On a cold, overcast afternoon off the coast of Brazil, one of the seamen pointed off into the distance and cried, "Look, mates, on the port side!"

We looked and there he was. Mopey Duke, the great white whale.

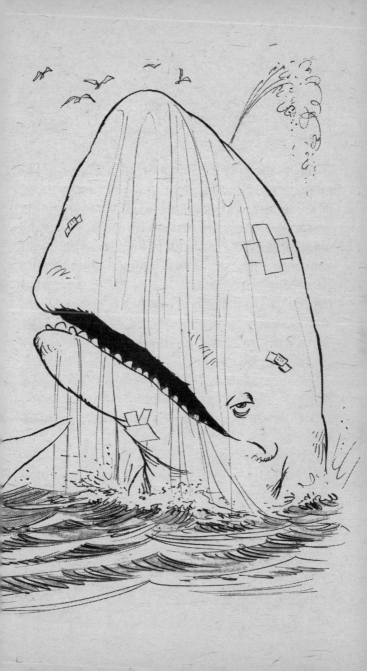

He was truly a magnificent creature. He measured at least 65 feet in length and was as white as the billowing surf he churned up in his wake. Somehow there was an aura of dignity about this sleek, graceful beast, and you could sense an air of almost human intelligence permeating his being. We sailors responded deeply to this miracle of God in the only way we knew how.

"Kill him!" we screamed. "Kill the son of a bitch!"

We unleashed a fusillade of harpoons. Many of them found their marks in his flanks, while others he ripped to pieces with his cavernous jaws.

The battle raged for hours with Captain Aycrab lying on deck taking it all in with his wooden eyes.

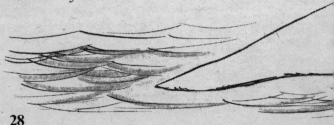

As I stared at the captain the enigmatic words of the venerable sage kept racing through my mind: "You will kill him single-headedly."

The great white whale was now a fearsome, thrashing beast in the last throes of life. The harpoons had taken their toll, but his indomitable spirit to live prevailed. With an herculean effort he maneuvered his gargantuan body towards the ship in one last crazed effort to destroy us all. We knew that one last well-directed blow was required to kill the whale and save our lives. But we were suddenly faced with heart-stopping reality. We had no more weapons!

As everyone aboard froze in fear and awaited our date with eternity, the great whale moved closer and closer.

Then something clicked in my mind. I knew what I had to do, and I did it.

I picked up the makeshift harpoon and launched it. And as he soared through the air, with the rope tied around his ankles, and his great, sharp, iron nose aimed straight and true for the heart of the mighty whale, a tiny smile creased the wooden mouth of Captain Aycrab.

The prophesy had come true!

The treasured reminiscences of a beloved schoolmaster

GOODBYE, MR.GREPPS

by James Miltown

It is hard to believe that today I am 85 years of age, and that well over 50 of those years have been spent as a school teacher.

While a world consumes itself with hatred and bloodshed, would you forgive an old man if he relaxes before his fire and pauses to jot down a few recollections of happier days in this, my humble book of memories? Perhaps a story or two depicting the humanity and decency of the teaching profession, an anecdote or two describing some of the warm, endearing qualities of students I have known, and finally a few words about the wonders of the educational system as it operates and functions today in a free world.

On second thought I have decided to write a book on jogging.

A tale of revolting pre-Revolutionaries, impure Puritans, moral debasement, and general messing around in the American colonies...

THE SCALLOPED LETTER

by Naspaniel Heartworn

One summer afternoon in Boston in the early days of the Massachusetts colony, a woman named Esther Prim appeared before a tribunal of church elders. She was charged with the second most horrible crime known to the Puritan Church: having sexual relations with a man other than your husband. The *first* most horrible crime, of course, was having sexual relations *with* your husband.

Her crime resulted in a child of sin, and the elders were repelled.

"What a foul deed!" said one of the elders.

"Disgusting!" said an elder elder.

"Unspeakable!" said a younger elder elder.

"Disgraceful!" said an elder younger elder elder.

"Feh!" said a Jewish elder.

As was the custom in pre- (and post-) American Revolutionary church trials, she was found guilty, and then the trial began. When it was over, Esther Prim stood before the court to hear the verdict.

Solemnly the eldest elder pronounced sentence on the luckless woman. "The court hath found the defendant guilty," he said.

"I do not accept that verdict," said the woman. "You said 'hath found,' and only Quakers say 'hath' instead of 'has.' I will not accept the verdict of a Quaker with an axe to grind."

"I am not a Quaker with an axe to grind!" the eldest elder said. "I am a Puritan with a lithp."

"That's one on you, thmartie," said another elder who also lisped.

"Before we pass sentence," said an elder, "you must reveal the name of the man who shared this despicable experience with you."

"Never!" said the haughty woman, who then added proudly, "And I do not consider it to be a despicable experience."

"How would you describe it?" asked an angry elder.

The woman thought for a moment. "Fair," she replied. "But you know what they say, even bad sex is good. And around here it's terrific."

This further infuriated the elders, who unfortunately had known nothing but terrific sex all their lives, and never really expected it to get any better.

And so sentence was passed on Esther. For twelve hours a day she was to stand on a scaffold in the center of the town square so that all who passed could heap scorn on her. And since the last delivery of scorn had arrived in early Spring, the elders reckoned the town had enough to sustain itself for 106 years, give or take a scoff.

In addition to all this, it was decided that Esther was to wear a letter "S" with scalloped edges, on the front of her gown over her chest, for the rest of her life.

"What does the letter 'S' stand for?" she asked.

"Sinner!" roared an elder. "It is a badge of shame to be worn by all who have committed your vile act, brought blasphemy to your community, and profaned, with an indelible scar of damnation, the entire Puritan faith."

"And why are the edges of the letters scalloped?" asked Esther.

"I don't know," said the elder, with a dreamy look in his eye. "It sort of highlights the rest of the ensemble and gives it some pizzazz."

The other elders nodded their agreement.

"Of course, a little lace on the fringes wouldn't hurt either," suggested another elder, but he was voted down.

Then the first elder turned wrathful again and said, "And now, Esther Prim, the sentence will be carried out, and you shall wait until the Avenging Angel comes to earth and carries you off to the dreaded abyss of Hell."

And so the sentence was carried out, and Esther Prim did indeed stand on the scaffold in the center of town, with the scalloped letter on her chest, while the citizens heaped scorn on her, and she waited for the Avenging Angel to come down to drag her off to the fiery abyss of Hell.

One day, during the second year of Esther's sentence, the elders gathered for a meeting. Suddenly one of the men rose to speak. He was a religious Puritan, a righteous citizen, and a reverent family man.

"Gentlemen," he said, "I have lived with a terrible secret for too long now. I must confess who it was that shared that despicable experience with Esther Prim."

The assemblage buzzed and leaned forward in anticipation.

The man paused for a moment. Then he screamed, "He did it! He did it!" and he pointed at a minister named Rev. Dummdolt.

He was *also* a devout fink!

"I saw them," he went on, "through a hole in the wall of the barn."

And a pious peeping Tom.

Rev. Dummdolt rose, and his voice trembling, addressed the audience. "Fellow elders," he said, "I am a minister of the Lord, and I have always led a most exemplary life. But even the noblest, the most devoted, and the most God-fearing of us is entitled to make one mistake."

The elders looked at each other. Then one spoke: "Rev. Dummdolt is right. Every man should be allowed to make one mistake, and he made his with Esther Prim."

"That's true," said another. "He made his with Esther Prim."

"And eleven others," Rev. Dummdolt added.

"Eleven others?" the elders gasped.

"But it was still the same mistake," the Reverend reminded them.

"Of course," the first elder repeated. "Every man should be allowed a mistake 12 times as long as it's the same one. Rev. Dummdolt is exonerated."

The other elders cheered.

Except one, who said, "But if everybody is allowed a mistake, what about Esther Prim?"

"You fool," said the first elder. "I said every *man*..."

And the others had to agree that he did.

The following morning in the center of the town square, Esther Prim and eleven other women stood on the scaffold with the scalloped letter "S" on their chests, and there they remained for many months to receive a goodly portion of the town's well-stocked scorn.

Then one day there was suddenly a flash of lightning and a clap of thunder in the sky. The townspeople were startled, and they had a premonition, and all at once a strange-looking figure in a cowl approached them, seemingly from out of nowhere. He walked to the center of the town, and pointing to the twelve women, he said in an awesome voice, as the sky crackled again, "I want them!"

The elders nodded solemnly. "We were expecting you," one of them said.

Then rounding up the women with the fateful letter "S" on their chests, the stranger in the cowl departed from the town as the elders stood by and silently prayed.

A short distance out of town Esther said to the figure, "Then you are truly the Avenging Angel from Hell's abyss?"

The figure shook his head. "I am Ezra Anson from Salem, Massachusetts. I own the Salem Turkeys."

And that night at the season's opener of the 1739 lacrosse season, the partisan Salem crowd was treated to the world's first bevy of cheerleaders. They were an instant success, and the beauty part of it all, as far as the owner was concerned, was that it didn't cost him a dime for their uniforms.

A very taut, crisp, fatalistic tale about two men desperately trying to find another man, and a famous writer desperately trying to find an ending for a short story...

THE KILLERDILLERS
by Earnest Hummingwords

Two men walked into Harry's Diner and sat down at the counter.

"What are you having?" Harry asked them.

"I don't know," said the first man. "I don't know what I'm having."

"What are you having?" Harry asked the second man.

"I'm having what he's having," said the second man.

"But he doesn't know what he's having," said Harry.

"When he does, I'll have it," said the second man.

"In other words," said Harry, "you want to have what he has as soon as he knows what he's having, but since he doesn't, he won't and you can't."

"Can't what?" asked the second man.

"Have what he doesn't know he's having," said Harry.

"Wait, he *can* have what I said I don't know I'm having," said the first man.

"How come?" asked Harry.

"Because now I know what I want," said the first man.

"What do you know you want," asked Harry, "which he can have now, that he couldn't have when you didn't?"

"I want veal chops with mashed potatoes and string beans, a side of cole slaw, and a cup of coffee and a piece of blueberry pie a la mode," said the first man.

"I'll have salisbury steak with brussel sprouts, carrots and peas, fried onion rings, a chocolate shake, and a brownie," said the second man.

"But I thought you were having what he's having," said Harry.

"I didn't know he was having *that*," said the second man. "And now that I do, I won't."

"Look," said the first man, "why don't you give us both meat loaf."

"With string beans, corn, and a kaiser roll?" asked Harry.

The men nodded.

"A cup of lentil soup and a dinner salad with Thousand Island dressing?"

The men nodded once more.

"And a cup of cocoa with whipped cream and some vanilla wafers?"

Again the men nodded.

"I don't have it," said Harry.

The first man reached over and grabbed Harry by the front of the shirt. "You're a smart boy," he said. "Isn't he a smart boy?" he asked the second man.

"He sure is a smart boy, all right," said the second man. "How come you don't have all that stuff, smart boy?"

"I don't know," said Harry. "I just don't know. I wish I did know, but I don't. Maybe you know."

"I don't know either, smart boy," said the second man. "Do you know?" he asked the first.

"I don't know," said the first man. "But maybe smart boy knows something else. Like where we can find an Albanian named Fornescu Zetts?"

"Why do you want to know if I can help you find the Albanian?" asked Harry.

"I don't know," said the first man. "But I do know we're gonna kill him. We just don't know why."

"But how can you kill a man if you don't know why you're gonna kill him?" asked Harry.

"Because we were hired by some men to kill him," said the first man. "And they know *everything*."

"Why do *they* want you to kill him?" asked Harry.

"Everything except *that*," said the first man.

"I'll be right back," said Harry.

"Where are you going?" asked the second man.

"I don't know," said Harry. But he really did.

Harry ran to the boarding house on the corner and burst into a room. The Albanian was lying in bed staring at the ceiling.

"Albanian," said Harry, breathlessly, "there's some men in my diner. They say they're gonna kill you, but they don't know why."

"I know," said the Albanian.

"They said they were hired by some men to kill you," said Harry, "and *they* don't know why they want you killed either."

"I know that too," said the Albanian. "Would you like to hear a story?"

"Yes," said Harry. But he really didn't know if he did.

"Many years ago," said the Albanian, "a young boy came to these shores from a foreign country. He was a penniless orphan and he sold newspapers. One day there was an accident and he saved the life of the Governor of Idaho, but in the same accident a famous racketeer was killed. Well, the Governor thought the boy was trying to kill him, not save his life, and the racketeer's mob thought the boy *had* killed *him*. So ever since then every cop and hood in the country has been searching for that boy."

"And you were that boy?" said Harry.

"No, I was the Governor of Idaho," said the Albanian.

"I don't believe it," said Harry.

"There's no reason why you should," said the Albanian. "I just made it up. You said you wanted to hear a story."

Suddenly a barrage of bullets crashed through the window and the Albanian slumped over in his bed.

"It's all over," said Harry, standing over the lifeless form. "Killed by two men who don't know why they killed him, hired by men who don't know why they paid to have him killed. And now a man is dead, and God only knows why."

"Not really," said God.

Aone-word condensation of...

THE COMPLETE WORKS OF THE MARQUIS DE SADE

OUCH!!

A classic short story about a man who puts his foot in his mouth and sells his soul to a heel...

THE DEVIL AND SAMUEL FENSTER

by Steven Brith Binay

Not too long ago there lived a farmer named Jason Groan. He was a decent man and he tried hard, but he had all sorts of problems. He suffered and struggled, and he was always living from hand to mouth. And considering what farmers do with their hands, you can well understand *one* of his problems.

Anyway, while his neighbors thrived and prospered, for some reason Jason just kept going downhill. His crops were terrible, his cows gave sour milk, his hens laid rotten eggs, and he had the only rooster in the world who slept until noon. But it didn't really end there because nothing seemed to go right for the farmer in his home life either.

For one thing his wife who was an awful nag when they first married, turned into an excellent one over the years. Then of course there was his son, who was so totally inept and was such a bore that sheep used to yawn at him on dates. And as for the farmer's daughter... Not only couldn't Jason marry her off, but traveling salesmen took one look at her and just kept traveling.

Then one day Jason decided he had had it. It all began when the rooster woke him up at 3:00 in the afternoon. "I can't understand why he gets up so late," said Jason's wife. "He goes to sleep with the chickens."

"There's one reason right there," said Jason.

From there on in, as usual, the day was one disaster after another. It culminated finally with the arrival of the veterinarian, who informed Jason that his ox had a double hernia, and then he presented him with an outlandish bill.

"Things just can't get any worse!" roared Jason, throwing the bill to the ground.

"I'm afraid they can," said the vet, patting the enormous beast on one of its sore flanks. "Wait till you see how much a truss is going to cost you for this mother."

On his way to Ox Trusserama in the town shopping mall, Jason suddenly stopped on the road and shouted to no one in particular, "I'd give *anything* for a change in luck. So help me, I'd even sell my soul to the devil."

All at once a horse and buggy appeared, riding rapidly up to Jason and knocking him off his feet. A stranger got out of the buggy. He had a frightening look in his eyes, two small horns on the sides of his head, and his teeth were white and incredibly sharp. Jason took one look at him and froze.

"Oh my God!" said Jason.

"Not even close," said the stranger.

"You mean you're...?" Jason gasped.

The stranger nodded. Then taking out a piece of paper and a pen, he said, "Very well, here's the deal. I'm going to trade you seven years of incredible wealth and enormous riches for your poor, miserable, worthless soul."

Jason signed the contract, which sure enough guaranteed him incredible wealth and enormous riches in exchange for an option on his miserable, worthless soul. This done the devil left immediately to moonlight on the West Coast, where, commensurate with his trading talents, he served as part-time General Manager for the San Francisco Forty-Niners.

During the next seven glorious years everything went right for Jason. He had nothing but bountiful crops. His cows not only gave the finest milk, but low-fat from one udder, non-fat from the other udder, and buttermilk which was utter butter from still another udder.

And that wasn't all. Jason's home and land were featured in a 17 page spread in *Farm Beautiful* magazine. His wife became so charming that a TV producer signed her on as Charlie's fourth—and oldest—angel. His son suddenly turned dynamic and was named "Mr. Excitement" by a flock of prize merino sheep in Laramie, Wyoming. And finally, and most gratifying of all to Jason, after a hectic and rocky romance that gathered headlines on four continents, his daughter married Hugh Hefner and in the process broke Warren Beatty's heart.

Well obviously things couldn't be better for Jason, until one day when he looked at the calendar and realized, to his horror, that his time was up in a few days, and the devil would be there soon to collect on his contract.

"I'm so miserable," said Jason to his wife as he sobbed and wrung his hands. "Any day now the devil is going to take all this away from me and gain control over my immortal soul. What am I going to do? What am I going to do?"

His wife turned to him and said, "Look, schmuck, stop bugging me and go see a lawyer." (While she *was* quite charming these days, she *did* have occasional lapses.)

At any rate Jason thought her idea was a good one, and he immediately caught a plane for Juneau, Alaska, to talk to Samuel Fenster, who was far and away the greatest defense attorney in the country (actually there was a lawyer in Jersey City who was just as good, but he wasn't far and away).

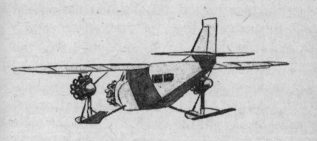

Well Samuel Fenster agreed to handle the case, and he returned with Jason to his home to await the arrival of the devil. Sure enough at the stroke of midnight on the appointed day, the devil arrived to collect on his business deal.

Jason informed him that he was not going to give up without a fight, and he suggested a court trial. To his delight the devil accepted the offer. But he did make one condition. *He* would select the judge and jury. And he did. And what a selection it was.

A short while later the jury filed into the room, all doomed souls from the deepest bowels of hell. Never before had so many unspeakable monsters gathered together in one room on earth, and when Jason found out who they were, a cold shudder darted up and down his spine.

The jury consisted of a former used car dealer; an ex-television repair man; a one-time garage mechanic; a former oil sheikh from Libya; an ex-adman who created the first commercial comparison test; a one time real estate broker from Beverly Hills; a former surgeon who handled nothing but medicare cases; two ex-ayatollahs; and three former TV network presidents.

Jason was understandably distraught. "I don't have a chance with this despicable vermin," he moaned. "I'm doomed."

But his attorney patted his hand reassuringly and told him not to worry. There was no case on hell or earth that was too tough for the great Samuel Fenster, he reminded him.

Then the judge entered the room. "Who's that?" asked Jason.

"John Hancock," said the devil.

"I'm saved," said Jason, a smile breaking out on his face. "Any man who signed the Declaration of Independence *must* be on the side of good."

"I told you you have nothing to worry about," said Samuel.

"He was also an insurance man," the devil reminded him.

"Oh my God," said Jason, collapsing in a chair. "I'm a goner."

"You sure are," said Samuel. But he agreed to do the best he could.

The judge rapped his gavel and the trial began.

The devil rose. "It's an open and shut case," he said.

Then he opened his attaché case, took out the contract, held it up in the air, put it back, and shut the case.

As he smiled evilly and sat down, Samuel got up to face the jury.

"Gentlemen of the jury," he said, "I realize that you all represent the very dregs of humanity. You are without question the most wretched, the most contemptible..."

"Objection, your honor," said the devil. "This is highly illegal procedure."

"Sustained," said the judge. "The defense will refrain from trying to flatter the jury. Please stick to the facts."

Samuel nodded and addressed the jury again. He told them that no matter where they came from now and regardless of their reputations, they must remember that this trial was being held in the United States of America, and must be conducted under the rules of American jurisprudence.

"We're aware of that, counsel," said the judge impatiently. "Now please proceed."

And so summoning up his vast courtroom experience and adhering slavishly to the procedures that had made the United States legal system the envy of the free world and tyrants alike, Samuel opened his historic defense.

"Now then," he began, "regarding this alleged contract…"

The devil leaped to his feet.

"*Alleged* contract?" he screamed, ripping open his attaché case and holding the paper aloft. "How can you call this an *alleged* contract?"

Samuel sighed and turned to the judge. "Your honor," he said, "you must know that under American law *everything* is alleged, unless it is unalleged. In which case it is an alleged unallegement."

Then to prove his point, he quoted from D.E. Doope *versus* the Alleged D.E. Doope, U.S. Court of Appeals, 1923.

The judge had to admit that Samuel did indeed prove his point.

"And yet, your honor," Samuel went on, "in the face of all this unshakable evidence, the alleged devil still insists that his contract is valid."

Now the devil was livid. "*Alleged* devil!" he roared.

But there was no stopping the brilliant attorney. Utilizing remarkable courtroom expertise, sprinkled liberally with a large number of "whomsoevers" and "whatsoevers" and "ipso factos" and "habeas corpuses" and all the other marvelous expressions that had made this country great, Samuel Fenster not only succeeded in having Jason's contract declared void, but also convinced the jury to declare the plaintiff a fraud for impersonating a devil.

"And in addition to all this," the judge concluded somberly, "the court hereby fines the alleged devil $25,000 for driving an uninsured horse and buggy while wilfully running into the defendant on the road to the shopping mall seven years ago, and causing severe whiplash."

There was pandemonium in the room, and Jason leaped up and down for joy, warmly clasping his attorney's hand.

Bitterly the plaintiff turned to Samuel and said, "So I'm an alleged devil, am I? I'll show you."

"What are you going to do?" asked Samuel, chuckling. "Turn me into a bull-frog?"

Whereupon everyone in the courtroom laughed.

"When will you learn," Samuel continued, "that the decision of a United States court is binding and unbreakable?"

The courtroom cheered.

"When will you ever grasp the fact," he went on, "that you *were* an imposter—rivit—that you *are* an imposter—rivit—and that you always *will* be an imposter—rivit rivit."

With that Samuel flicked his tongue three feet into the air, caught a fly, and then hopped off to a lily pad in a nearby pond, where he croaked.

Once again American justice had triumphed.

In which the greatest writer of them all recounts the story of the greatest Roman of them all in the rise and fall of

JULIUS SEESAW

by William Spakefair

E(A street in Rome)
nter the conspirators, Kasha, Cautious, Brutish, Hepatitus, Diabetus, Bronchitus, *and* Croup.)

Kasha. Marry, comrades, and ay verily.

Cautious. Odds bodkins.

Brutish. Forsooth.

Hepatitus. Nay, vouchsafe.

Diabetus. Fain, fie, and foo.

Bronchitus. Foo, fie, and fain.

Croup. Tilly-fally.

Kasha. Ya, varlets.

Cautious. How now, ill met, methinks.

Brutish. Methinks too, prithee, lief.

(Exeunt all, having just agreed to assassinate Julius Seesaw for being too ambitious, but owing to the author's strange language, the audience doesn't know this yet. Come to think of it, for the same reason, neither do the conspirators. Enter Julius Seesaw and his entourage, as a sudden storm hits the city.)

Seesaw. What evil weather befouls Rome. Methinks it is snowing.

Enter *Mock Agony.*

Agony. Hail, Seesaw.

Seesaw. Oh, methought it was snow.

Agony. No, when I say Hail Seesaw, I mean… never mind.

Seesaw. A pox on the weather. It hath spoiled my toga.

Agony. The Roman Cleaning Emporium hath a special one-day toga service, my lord. "In at IX, Out by IV."

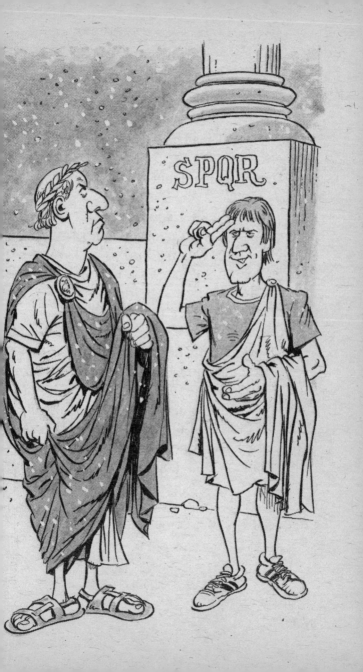

Seesaw. Good. I shall take the street north to the cleaners.

    They start to exeunt north. Enter a *man in a cowl.*

Man in cowl. Sooth… sooth.

Seesaw. Who sayeth sooth, when I say north?

Agony. A soothsayer, my lord.

Seesaw. Fie on soothsayers. I go north to the cleaners anyway.

Man in cowl. Beware the ides of March.

    (He exeunts.)

Seesaw. What hath he said this time, Agony?

Agony. Methinks he said, beware the dyes and starch.

Seesaw. Methinks he said something else. Methinks thou dost not hear too well. Perhaps thine ears have gone bad. Wouldst thou like some Romans and countrymen to lend you *theirs?*

Man in cowl. *(off-stage, from whence he has exeunted)* No, that comes after. *After.*

Seesaw. What means he by after, Agony? After *what?*

Agony. Forget it, my lord.

    Enter the conspirators, concealing knives in their tunics.

Seesaw. Behold, my loyal subjects and dearest friends join me. Even though it is snowing, this is my lucky day.

Man in cowl. (off-stage) Wanna bet?

Conspirators. (All) Hail, Seesaw.

Seesaw. Snow, schmucks. *Snow!* But no matter, it is still a glorious day. Come, thou shalt all accompany me whilst I greet the beautiful queen of Egypt, Cleohotcha, who awaits me on a barge. Oh how my heart pounds for her. Oh, I am in ecstasy. Oh… oh…

    (All draw knives.)

Seesaw. Oh-oh.

(All raise their knives and attack Seesaw.*)*

Kasha. Marry, comrades, and ay verily.

Cautious. Odds bodkins.

Brutish. Forsooth.

Hepatitus. Nay, vouchsafe.

Diabetus. Fain, fie, and foo.

Bronchitus. Foo, fie, and fain.

Croup. Tilly-fally.

    (All stab Seesaw, *but because of the language, they still don't know why. He falls.)*

Seesaw. (beckoning Brutish *to his side)* Et tu, Brutish? Thou wert my dearest companion. Did we not share a lifetime together? Was I not like a brother to thee? Hast thou not one decent thing to say to me after all this?

Brutish. Have a nice day.

Kasha. Methinks Brutish's heart is not in this.

    *(*Seesaw *dies)*

Agony. What a foul morning. What dark deeds.

(Enter citizens of Rome, who gasp at the sight of Seesaw.)

1st Citizen. Speak, Agony. Thou must speak at Seesaw's funeral.

2nd Citizen. Ay, thou art the greatest orator in Rome.

3rd Citizen. We await thy priceless words as the meadow awaits the precious rain.

Agony. Ay, I shall speak. And this is what I have to say…Friends, Romans, countrymen, lend me your ears…

1st Citizen. Nay! Nay! Not *that* old chestnut.

2nd Citizen. Every idiot in school knoweth *that* one.

3rd Citizen. Borrrrrrring!

Agony. Very well. How is this?…

(And so instead Agony *tells them a wonderful story about an Irishman, a Polack, and a Jew trapped in a Turkish bath, and he ends up to thunderous applause. He waves aside the applause.)*

Agony. Citizens, a final word about our beloved Seesaw. I have read his will, and he hath left everything he owns to the people of Rome. To his wife he hath left his home and gold. To the Senate he hath left his arbors and vineyards, and to the masses he hath left his farmlands.

1st Citizen. What hath he left for you, Agony?

Agony. For me? Nought but a small gift, which I would gladly return if by some miracle the noble Seesaw could be brought back to life.

(A barge sails by on the Tiber. A woman on board waves.)

Seesaw. (rises) Cleohotcha! I shall be right there!

Citizens. (shocked) My God, look! Seesaw still lives!

Agony. Not for long!

(He grabs a nearby knife and stabs Seesaw dead. He runs to the water and dives in.)

Agony. Coming, oh precious gift of the Nile!

Soothsayer. (enters) Beware the tides of March!

Agony. (swimming furiously) I'll take my chances!

The heartwarming and stomach-turning story of peasant life in China...

THE GOODLY EARTH
by Beryl Pox

One day in a small village in China, a man named Worn Lung took unto him a bride. She was a beautiful, voluptuous creature named Oh-Man, and she was the answer to Worn Lung's most impossible dream. Not only could she carry 200 pounds of fire wood on her back and walk 300 miles to Shanghai for groceries, but she could go five weeks without water. All his life Worn Lung had dreamed of owning a camel, and in China of course—until now—that had been impossible.

Home life was extremely democratic in the house of Worn Lung and Oh-Man (as it was all over China). The wife did all the work, going non-stop at 50 miles an hour, and the husband did nothing before and after the age of 50. In short, marriage was a 50-50 proposition.

And so time passed, with Oh-Man tending to all the household chores, catering to her husband's every need, fetching him his opium pipe and slippers, and presenting him with a new baby every nine months. Worn Lung had loved his growing family, but somehow the children just weren't coming fast enough for him. And thus, ever the dutiful wife, in time Oh-Man found ingenious ways of having babies more rapidly: first, a new one every six months, then one every three months, and finally a baby every two weeks (she had recently taken out a subscription to the International Edition of *Reader's Digest*).

Worn Lung was a wonderful husband and father with perhaps one noticeable flaw—a terrible sense of humor. But Oh-Man learned to tolerate it. As, for example, the time he suggested that the eldest of their 27 daughters, Woo-Woo, might get a job checking coats at a café in Canton.

Knowing, of course, what was coming next, Oh-Man gritted her teeth and said dutifully, "Why do you think Woo-Woo should get a job checking coats at a café in Canton?"

Whereupon Worn Lung giggled and said, "What's the matter, you never heard of a Chinese Checker?"

As he exploded with laughter and rolled all over the floor, she stifled a groan and went to the linen closet to pick up some towels and pillow cases, and then as an afterthought on the way out, she had another baby.

Soon days became weeks, weeks became months, and months became years (it seemed that *all* China was now subscribing to *Reader's Digest*). And then the Worn Lungs were hit with their first big family crisis.

"Most exalted husband," said Oh-Man one day (their years of incredible intimacy had emboldened her to address him now familiarly), "I have just received some disturbing news from school regarding our 38th son."

"You mean our future orator?" said Worn Lung. "The boy with the tongue of silver."

She nodded. "Yes, our son, Hi-Yo. It pains me to inform you that he was caught red-handed in the Boy's Room yesterday *not* smoking opium."

"What?" screamed Worn Lung, smashing his own opium pipe on the floor (he had been in a sour mood anyway, having just returned from a bad trip to Mars, Uranus, and Secaucus, New Jersey). "Doesn't he know that *all* decent, God-fearing people in China smoke opium? What is it with children today?"

Then he summoned for the boy.

"Why? Why have you done this?" asked a highly distraught Worn Lung, as his son, Hi-Yo, stood before him shamefaced.

"I'm sorry, Father," said Hi-Yo. "It's just that a lot of kids in school are not smoking opium these days. You can't *believe* how many. I guess I just wanted to be part of the crowd."

As Worn Lung agonized over this horrendous turn of events, his whole world crumbling around him, Oh-Man tried to soothe her husband's feelings. "Don't be so hard on him," she said. "Try to understand. He just got caught up in good company."

But Worn Lung was in no mood for compromise. "Listen to me, young man," he said. "You're going to start smoking opium full time, and *at once.* No pussy-footing. It's the only way."

"You mean…?" said Hi-Yo ominously.

Worn Lung nodded his head gravely and said, "Hot turkey."

As a now contrite Hi-Yo left the room puffing desperately on one of his father's opium pipes, Oh-Man said, "It won't be easy for him starting in just like that."

"Of course not," said her husband. "He'll just have to learn how to cope with those terrible attack symptoms."

Then a smile creased his face, and a twinkle lit up his eyes, and Oh-Man feared what was coming next. As it turned out, her fears were soon realized.

"I was just thinking," said Worn Lung, "perhaps Hi-Yo should not become an orator. Perhaps instead he should be a barber."

Oh-Man winced, but ever dutiful, she fed him the line he so earnestly desired. "Why should he be a barber?" she asked, bracing herself.

"You never heard of the China Clipper?" he said, erupting in uncontrollable paroxysms of laughter.

Unable to face up to that one, Oh-Man fled to the pantry, where she immediately gave birth to twins. Then in a defiant gesture, she decided to punish her husband, and put them back.

And so life went on peacefully in the little Chinese village, until one year when the forces of nature were suddenly unleashed against the family with all their fury. Famine, pestilence, floods, and finally one morning, while standing in their fields, Worn Lung and Oh-Man saw a dangerous black cloud approaching them. "Oh my God," she said. "It's the 17-year locusts!"

Millions of the deadly insects swooped down on the village, destroying everything in their path. Plants, trees, houses, and most horrible of all, whole families of their neighbors. In a matter of minutes the locusts had devoured the Wong family, the Fong family, and their closest and dearest friend, Chuck-Ee and the entire Gong family.

Then just as quickly the insects disappeared. Sighing with relief, the couple once again tried to pick up the pieces of their lives. "Thank God they're gone," said Oh-Man, "and they won't be back for a long time."

But a short while later, to their great dismay, the black cloud formed once more in the distance and began to swoop down on the village again.

"They're not supposed to return for 17 years!" screamed Oh-Man. "Why have they come back in thirty minutes?"

Then all at once that familiar impish grin crossed the face of Worn Lung and he said, "Don't forget, Woman, they have just eaten Chinese, and a half hour after you've…"

"If you say what I think you're going to say," warned Oh-Man, "I'll kill you."

But he did, and she did.

She was brought to trial, and the jury deliberated for only a minute and a half before returning with their verdict: "Very, very, very, very justifiable homicide."

A story of social injustice in 19th century France which shows that man's inhumanity to man is almost as cruel as having to wade through 1,222 endless pages of the original book...

LES MESSYRABBLES
by Victim Hugoe

It was the year 1796 and conditions in France were terrible. There was poverty and misery everywhere. The plague was taking its toll of the populace, and people were dropping like flies. It was pathetic to see grown men fall off walls on their backs and try to roll over and spread their non-existent wings. But these were heartbreaking times.

And so it happened, amidst all this, that a man named Johnvalve Jean stole a loaf of bread to help feed his starving sister. Unfortunately the act was witnessed by Inspector Camembert, one of the most dedicated gendarmes on the entire French police force, who immediately gave chase. For weeks, with Camembert in hot pursuit, Johnvalve slogged through the sewers of Paris. Not so much because that was the best escape route, but because considering the conditions of the streets, he needed the fresh air.

Johnvalve managed to elude the dogged inspector in the sewers, but as luck would have it, just as he reached his sister's house and handed her the bread, Camembert appeared and clapped him in chains.

The sister was very upset. "I appreciate all your trouble, Johnvalve," she said. "But you know you have done a foolish thing."

"I know my dear sister," said Johnvalve, as he was being led away, "but still I would do it for you again."

"The hell you will," she said, throwing the bread in his face. "When I ask for pumpernickel, I want pumpernickel!"

Scarred around his cheeks and eyes for life (14-day-old bread can be a deadly weapon) Johnvalve was dragged off to court, and was sentenced to 19 years in prison. He gratefully thanked the judge, knowing full well that if this weren't his first offense, they would have thrown the book at him.

Life in prison was a harsh and grueling experience for Johnvalve. Especially since he had to share a cell with some of the most notorious criminals in France. Men like Michel Pommedeterre, a depraved bran muffin swiper, and Pierre Oiseau, a compulsive egg bagel thief. And then of course he was always haunted by the memory of his former cell-mate Henri Fromage, who years before was sent to the guillotine for the cruel and premeditated theft of a toasted bialy from the prison officer's mess.

Finally, in 1815, after serving his sentence, Johnvalve was given ten francs and a suit of clothes, and was released. He then began a long and painful trek through the country, trying to start a new life for himself.

It was a painful journey for him because the winter was bitter cold, people were unfriendly towards ex-convicts, and it was very difficult walking without shoes (French prison rules were very strict in those days. Released prisoners received ten francs and a suit of clothes and that's *it*).

A short while later Johnvalve met Police Inspector Camembert again in the streets of Paris. It was a traumatic experience for him.

Rapidly his memory raced back in time, and all his senses were reawakened. After 19 years, he could still see the gendarme slogging through the sewers after him. He could still feel his hot breath on his neck. He could still hear him saying, "I shall get you, Johnvalve Jean." But above all, he could still smell him. French justice was very powerful in those days. So were French sewers.

"So, Johnvalve Jean," said Camembert, "we meet again. It is true that you are a free man now, but our paths will cross again one day. Once a criminal, always a criminal."

Just then a pickpocket ran up to Johnvalve, stole his ten francs, and fled.

Johnvalve was beside himself, but since he was also beside Camembert, he shouted at him, "You are a police officer! Why don't you apprehend that man?"

"Don't bother me," said Camembert, running off in the other direction. "You *know* I'm on the bread squad." And to prove his point, three blocks away he captured Louis Cochon, a man wanted in seven provinces for flagrant onion roll theft.

Despite the cruel shake he had received from society, Johnvalve nevertheless put his nose to the grindstone and his shoulder to the wheel, and in time he became a very successful business tycoon, cornering the entire grindstone and wheel industry in all France. He was now a wealthy and respected man. But something was missing from his life and he wasn't happy.

One day he was approached on the street by a miserable, unkempt woman. "Kind sir," she said, "I hate to bother such a grand gentleman like yourself, but I am in a good deal of trouble."

"Who are you?" Johnvalve asked her gently.

"My name is Fantan, and I am ashamed to tell you that I am a rotten prostitute," she said.

Johnvalve, who had heard of such women, but who had never met one, was appalled.

"Do you mean to tell me," he said, in disgust, "that you actually sell your body for money?"

"Oh no, sir," she said. "I don't sell it. I give it away."

Johnvalve nodded sadly. "You *are* a rotten prostitute," he agreed.

Frightened and embarrassed the poor woman ran away.

But the following day she left her illegitimate daughter, Coquette, in a laundry basket on Johnvalve's doorstep. While he sympathized with the poor woman, Johnvalve considered the act to be cruel and inexcusable. After all, one does not abandon one's own flesh and blood in a tiny laundry basket. Particularly if the child is 15 years old.

With the aid of some workmen and a pry and a lever, Johnvalve succeeded in dislodging the child from the basket, and he adopted her.

The years flew by, Coquette blossomed, and aside from an occasional back problem, especially when the weather was damp, she turned into a beautiful, healthy young woman.

Now Johnvalve's life was complete. His adopted daughter gave him the fulfillment he so desperately craved, and he had all he could wish for.

His business prospered. He continued to expand, opening grindstone and wheel factories all over Europe. He employed thousands of people, whom he always treated with kindness and compassion. He gave out generous bonuses, vacations, and a special gold watch to all employees who had been with him for 25 hours—or less.

Despite all this, some employees still complained about long working hours. And so Johnvalve originated the five day week. From that moment on, he eliminated Mondays and Thursdays from the Gregorian Calendar.

Then in later years when people began to miss those two days, he not only reinstated them as paid holidays, but added an eighth day to the week—Sophieday—which he named after his blessed mother. He was that kind of a man.

In addition to all this, he built hospitals, convalescent homes, donated millions of francs to charity, and was being strongly considered for beatification as the first living saint in history (and he wasn't even Catholic).

Then in the year 1840 the greatest honor of his life was bestowed upon him. He was ordained Pope of the Holy See (and he still wasn't Catholic). While he was somewhat disappointed about his sainthood being delayed (he was still one miracle short), he accepted the Papal crown with humility and dignity.

A special banquet commmemorating this momentous event was held for him at the Vatican, and flanked at the table by his step-daughter Coquette, who had recently married the Emperor of Austria, and his sister, the newly crowned Queen of Roumania, he thanked the audience of churchmen and other distinguished worshipers, pledging his life to wiping out war and poverty and putting an end to all communicable respiratory diseases.

When he finished his speech to thundering applause, he smiled, blessed the audience, then chuckled and said, "And now, everybody eat."

His sister picked up her croissant and said to him, "This looks delicious, Johnvalve. But I can't very well eat it dry. You know what I like on croissants."

Picking up his knife, he leaned over to another table and filled the knife. Suddenly a hand seized his wrist. "Aha," said a voice, "first you steal bread, and now it's butter. Will it *never* end, Your Holiness?"

With a gasp Johnvalve found himself staring into the face of Police Inspector Camembert, newly appointed to the International Dairy Squad.

Johnvalve sighed, rose to his feet, and said to his sister, "I realize what I have done, but still I would do it for you again."

"The hell you will," said his sister, throwing the butter in his face. "When I ask for jam, I want jam!"

Then lifting his Papal robes, and with Inspector Camembert in hot pursuit, Pope Johnvalve the First headed for the sewers of Rome.

An American classic about poor, oppressed Oklahoma sharecroppers who can only unleash their full fury against life's injustices after drinking cheap, homemade wine...

THE
WRATH
OF
GRAPES
by John Steinfull

It was the year 1934 and conditions in the United States were terrible. There was poverty and misery everywhere. The depression was taking its toll of the populace, and people were dropping like flies. It was pathetic to see grown men fall off walls on their backs and try to roll over and spread their nonexistent wings. (Author's Note: If you object to my stealing from "Les Messyrabbles," take a look some time at the way Carl Sandburg ripped off Walt Whitman).

If things were bad all over the country, they were even worse in Oklahoma. A severe drought had seized the land, the state was in a sea of dust, and there wasn't a drop of water to be found for hundreds of miles around. Children were forced to brush their teeth with lentil soup, sharecroppers had to irrigate their fields with ginger ale, and a common affliction among patients at Tulsa General Hospital was Ovaltine on the knee.

And so, in this most trying of times, a young man named Tim Toad was released from prison in Oklahoma City and returned to his miserable, ramshackled home, with its parched land and dried-out wells.

"Was it real tough in prison, Son?" asked Maw Toad.

"Only the last two years when I was in solitary," said Tim. "They had me on nothing but bread and celery tonic."

"You poor dear," said Maw, embracing him, as tears of Hawaiian Punch filled her eyes. "But the important thing is, we're all together again."

"You'll help me till the soil, Son," said Paw Toad. "Wait till you see how nice the garbage crops are comin' up, and we got a bumper harvest of dry mud this year."

Paw Toad was only a poor dirt farmer, but he was proud.

"Maw, Paw, everybody listen to me," said Tim. "This land is dead and we're bustin' through the walls of this rotten house. We gotta do somethin' about it. Our family's gettin' larger every day."

"I got an idea," said Tim's younger brother, Winslow. "Why don't Paw get a condominium?"

"Mind your dirty mouth," said Maw. "You *know* we don't use them things. We're Catholic."

Whereupon she washed his mouth out with soap and prune juice.

"I ain't talkin' about another home around here," said Tim, walking with Maw and Paw Toad through the dust that enveloped their miserable farm land. "I'm talkin' about movin' out of the state. I'm talkin' about goin' to California."

"What?" shrieked Paw. "Leave our native land? Never!"

"Paw," said Tim, "look at all this misery we're livin' in. Tell me one good thing about Oklahoma."

Paw thought for a moment and then said, "I don't know, I kind-a like the way the wind comes sweepin' cross the plain."

"That ain't no wind," said Tim. "It's a God-damn sandstorm!"

"Hush your mouth, Son," said Maw. "Are you tryin' to tell us that the wavin' wheat don't sure smell sweet?"

"Okay, okay," said Tim grudgingly. "But only when the wind comes right before the rain."

"Aha," said Maw triumphantly.

"But it ain't rained here in nine years," Tim reminded her.

"Son, listen to me," said Paw, seizing him by the shoulders, "this is your land as well as ours." Then he snickered and winked as he jostled Tim with his elbow. "I remember how in the good old days, you and that gal you were sweet on... what's her name?"

Tim thought for a while and then said nostalgically, "Oh yeah, my honey lamb..."

"Right," said Paw dreamily. "Remember how every night your honey lamb and you would sit alone and..."

"I don't wanna hear about it!" shouted Maw, holding her ears. "Don't tell me! Don't tell me!"

"Maw," said Tim, "all we did was *talk*."

"Sure, *talk*," said Paw, impishly winking and jostling Tim again. "All they did was talk." And he snickered again.

"Okay," said Tim. "Maybe every once in a while we'd watch a hawk makin' lazy circles in the sky. But that's as far as it went."

"And that's why we gotta stay," said Maw. "This is our home. It'll always *be* our home. We'll never leave."

Then Maw looked off into the distance. "Look, Son," she said. "There's a hawk up there right now makin' lazy circles in the sky. Wait a minute. I do declare, he seems to be carryin' off somebody. Who is that girl? She looks familiar."

"It's my honey lamb!" shouted Tim, running toward the flying bird. "He's carryin' off my honey lamb! And that ain't no hawk! It's a vulture!"

"Grab your things, Paw," said Maw. "We're leavin' Oklahoma."

"You kiddin', Maw?" said Paw. "You *know* we belong to the land, and the land we belong to is..."

But Maw was already in the house half-packed.

That afternoon the Toad family packed their few meager belongings on the back of Paw's battered pickup truck, and they headed West. Making the trip were Tim Toad, Maw Toad, Paw Toad, Grandmaw Toad, Grandpaw Toad, and all the children, including Winslow Toad, Lucie Toad, Rosie Toad, Noel Toad, Barney Toad, as well as the family's two pet toads, Toad Toad and Harry Hennessey (Harry might have only been a toad, but he was fiercely independent).

On the road with them were many other families from Oklahoma, also making the arduous voyage westward, and as they traveled from state to state, they were received with the same kind of greeting Americans always reserve for poor, miserable oppressed people who look to this wonderful country for salvation: "ECCH!"

From then on these people were known as "Ecchies," and somehow the name stuck.

Words just can't describe the incredible misery the Ecchies experienced during their trip. 5 6 3 2 7 4 9 8...(Come to think of it, neither can numbers.) Suffice it to say, it was an agonizing ordeal for the Toad family. They sweltered during the day and froze at night. Food was almost non-existent, and they were forced to live on cactus plants (and if you think it's easy sleeping all curled up with thousands of spines sticking in your body, you're sadly mistaken). Then one night, after Lucie Toad was almost raped by a passing oversexed porcupine, the family decided to switch to Holiday Inns.

Finally, after being ravaged by disease, wracked with illness, and Grandpaw Toad had gone to his Maker (a body shop outside of Provo, Utah—people were too poor in those days to have children in the manner we know and love) everything suddenly changed. They had reached California.

The filth and the poverty and the parched land they had known for so long had vanished. They found themselves traveling through green fields, picture post card mountains, and lush valleys. "I believe this is a fairyland," said Tom. And when they drove past the bars of West Hollywood, he *knew* it was.

In no time they were face to face with all the wonders of nature and man that had made California what it was. Among other things they saw a Tire Man sixty feet tall. They saw an enormous doughnut, three stories high. They passed a restaurant that was shaped like a man's hat. They drove by Our Lady of the Eternal Tan, and many other houses of worship. And throughout it all they were confronted by thousands of blond, bronzed men and women walking in and out of banks, hospitals, and funeral homes carrying surfboards and continually pleading with them to have a nice day.

"Maw, Paw, everybody," cried Tim, "we have seen California, and we now know where our future lies."

And they all cheered, "you're doin' great Oklahoma, Oklahoma *okay!*"

A few days later they were back in the filth and the poverty and the parched land of home, just in time to pick up 26 tickets to catch Oklahoma play Oklahoma State in the Dust Bowl.

Part One of a two part condensation of

WAR
AND
PIECE
by Leo Tolstoy

BOOM!!